HAYNES EX
SEX

Owners' Workshop Manual

© Haynes Publishing • Written by **Boris Starling**

Published in January 2020

A catalogue record for this book is available from the British Library

ISBN 978 1 78521 653 4

Haynes Publishing, Sparkford, Yeovil,
Somerset BA22 7JJ, UK
Tel: +44 (0) 1963 440635
Website: www.haynes.com

Haynes North America, Inc.,
861 Lawrence Drive, Newbury Park,
California 91320, USA

Printed and bound in Malaysia

Cover image from Getty Images

Illustrations taken from the
Haynes Austin Maestro
Owners Workshop Manual

Written by **Boris Starling**
Edited by **Louise McIntyre**
Designed by **Richard Parsons**

Safety first!

In few other walks of life is the phrase 'safety first' so applicable as it is with sex. There's a reason few condom manufacturers ever go bust: people will always want to have sex (even if millennials are rumoured to be at it much less than previous generations were), and people will also always – well, almost always – want to avoid surprises which come in all shapes and sizes, from the bacterial via the parasitic to the all-too-human one which appears nine months later (rather embarrassing if you've forgotten, or never even knew, the father's name).

Working facilities

A bed is standard here. A single (90cm x 190cm) for students, who are young and limber enough not to need any bigger. A double (135cm x 190cm) for most people. A superking (180cm x 200cm) for those with lots of money and/or space, and perhaps little tolerance for their partner too. Other working facilities include but are not limited to: kitchen work surfaces, showers, laundry rooms, sofas, floors, gardens, alleyways, and for the very adventurous (and/or those with good lawyers) aisle 4 of the local Tesco's.

Contents

Introduction

Wet Wet Wet famously said that 'love is all around' (and kept saying it for what felt like a million years at number 1), but it's perhaps more accurate to say that sex is all around. It's in magazines and newspapers, on TV and film screens, and has even begun to spread in a small way onto the internet (or so I'm reliably informed).

On one hand, this is a good thing. For much of human history, sex has been seen as something to be performed out of duty, even to be endured: an obligation between married couples, a duty in terms of procreation. Such attitudes served only to undersell or negate sex for what it is, or at least what it can be: one of the most joyous, exciting, fulfilling and bonding experiences two (or more) humans can have.

On the other hand, this saturation comes at a price too. Sex can also be a source of great pain (emotional and physical), neuroticism and insecurity, and when we're bombarded with images of it night and day it can be easy to think that everyone is having (a) much more (b) much better sex than we are. And this is even before you factor in that they all seem to have perfect abs and apartments too, that the low lighting is designed to accentuate their sculpted cheekbones

rather than hide their love handles, and that they're never reduced to arguing over who sleeps in the wet patch. In turn, this can make people feel there's something wrong with them if their sex lives are not 100% amazing 100% of the time, and foist onto them artificial expectations of what they should be doing rather than what they actually are doing.

This is where Haynes Explains comes in. Not specifically to settle the wet-patch argument but to try and give a balanced view to the whole thing, to bust some myths (not least that we are all instinctively supposed to be perfect lovers), and hopefully to make you laugh a bit along the way too – for, let's face it, sex is inherently funny.

It's sweaty and undignified, it can produce noises and smells which wouldn't be out of place in a farmyard, and frankly it's amazing that more people don't stop halfway through, exclaim 'what must we look like?', and collapse into uncontrollable hysterics. It's a fairly absurd thing when all's said and done, so don't take it too seriously.

Dimensions, weights and capacities

Overall length

Of the penis .... 5–6 inches on average. No, mate, your ruler hasn't
.... been calibrated wrong. Trust us on this.

Of sex before male ejaculation ..... exactly 27.874% of how long a woman wishes it was.

Of the time a man spends looking
for sex of a given Friday night .... 5 hrs 32 mins.

Overall height

Of the tall stories men tell about
their sexual conquests .... roughly the same as the tallest skyscrapers.

Of an average woman in bare feet .... 5' 4"

Of an average woman in dominatrix heels 6' 2"

Of a man clinging to a windowsill while
his lover's husband expects her to share
his delight that he's back from work early... roughly six storeys above ground level.

Consumption

50mg of Viagra an hour before sexual activity. So plan ahead, chaps.
Viagra shouldn't be taken more than once a day, which let's face it is
pretty academic: chance would be a fine thing at your age.

Engine

Stroke.............. come on, this is too easy. This bit writes itself. Long, gentle strokes until
.... you're fully warmed up, and then you can start going quicker and harder.

Power .... 'Everything in the world is about sex except sex. Sex is about power.'
.... So said Oscar Wilde, the cynical old so-and-so.

Torque .... comes in various guises. Dirty torque, where one party informs the other
.... in graphic detail what they wish to do to them. Pillow torque, when both
.... parties whisper sweet post-coital nothings to each other. Big torque,
.... when the male exaggerates every aspect of the previous evening's
.... encounter to his mates in the pub the following night.

Redline .... Of a heart unused to vigorous physical activity, and therefore liable to
.... give out on the owner in flagrante.

Model differences

Humans come in two base models, female (XX) and male (XY). When it comes to sex, they could hardly be more different if they tried.

It's a popular trope that men think about sex every seven seconds, though where this figure actually came from is lost in the mists of time, as is the method by which it was calculated. 'Whatever you do, mate, don't think about sex. You got that? Think about

anything but sex.' Under those conditions, it may be that seven seconds is a conservative estimate. Women (probably) think about sex less often, if only because they actually have important things to worry about, but that doesn't necessarily mean that they're less interested in sex: just that they're more focused on quality than quantity. Few men would turn down the chance of more frequent sex: few women would turn down the chance of better sex.

A man and a woman sleep together. The next day, they go their separate ways and discuss it with a friend each. The woman's friend will want to know every last detail, not just of the sex itself but the build-up and aftermath too. The conversation on the male side will go as follows:

Friend: *You get laid?*
Man: *Yeah.*
Friend: *Nice one.*

This is a huge generalisation, of course (at Haynes Explains we know no other kind), but there is also much truth to it. Men tend to like sex for the way it makes their body feel; women tend to like sex for the way it connects them to their partner and fuels their emotions. (If this leads you to the man – shallow/

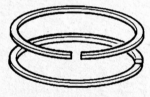

PUT A BIT OF LUBRICANT INSIDE THE RING...

... AND SLIDE IT ON, MAKING SURE IT FITS TIGHT BUT NOT TOO TIGHT

THIS REDUCES BLOOD FROM FLOWING BACK DOWN OUT OF THE PENIS

FIG 16•1 **LORD OF THE COCK RINGS, BY J. R. R. TOO-KEEN**

woman – deep corollary, we didn't say a thing.) Interestingly, studies of heterosexual couples in long-term relationships show the gap narrowing as the relationship becomes more secure, with men increasingly seeking sex by way of affirming that relationship and women increasingly enjoying the physical act secure in the stability of the relationship.

Other differences:

a) Men often enjoy a quick rush to sex. Women prefer a slower build-up.

b) Men are goal-oriented: they want to get to the orgasm. Women enjoy the journey there more and like to take the scenic route.

c) When being touched, men enjoy firmer pressure than women do.

d) Men are visual creatures, attracted to what they can see. Women use their other senses more, and pay attention to what a man says and how he smells, feels and tastes.

When it comes to model parts, of course, there are very noticeable differences.

The reasons for sex

People have sex for lots of reasons. One study of college students revealed 237 different reasons, but that's students for you. 'Waiting for *Neighbours* to start' is a pretty shoddy reason, let's face it. People have sex for physical reasons (attraction, pleasure, stress relief, curiosity, exercise), emotional reasons (love, commitment, gratitude, spiritual transcendence), insecurity reasons (self-esteem, approval-seeking, peer pressure, possession (of a partner, obviously, not Exorcist-style demonic possession: the Sexorcist, perhaps?)), or with specific goals in mind (making a baby, improve social status, gain revenge, make money). At a base level, however, as any sexologist will tell you (and yes, sexologist is a real job, they're hiring now), we have sex because we're programmed to do so.

Sexual behaviour, like the search for food, warmth and shelter, is wired into us as part of the need to ensure the survival of the species. So every time you knock boots, you're basically doing it for the collective. What a public-spirited lot you are.

XY parts

Male reproductive equipment
Penis (aka cock, knob, old chap, bellend, John Thomas, and 63,847 other names).

According to the Kama Sutra, penises come in three sizes: hare, bull and stallion. (This must presumably have been something of a blow to the bull, who after a hard day's work covering as many cows as possible might feel slightly aggrieved that its masculinity had not received greater recognition.) Certainly penises do come in a variety of shapes and sizes: the average is five or six inches long when erect, and its size when flaccid often bears little resemblance to its size when erect.

Around 45% of men are unhappy with the size of their penis, and of that 45% approximately 0.0% wish that it was smaller rather than larger. Lots of men still worry that they're too small even when they're well within average range or even higher.

The penis consists of several different parts:

a) **Foreskin.** A sleeve of flesh which covers the glans (see below). Often removed shortly after birth for cultural or religious reasons. Schoolboys with the surname 'Erskine Crum' wearily resign themselves to many years of being called 'Foreskin Bum'.

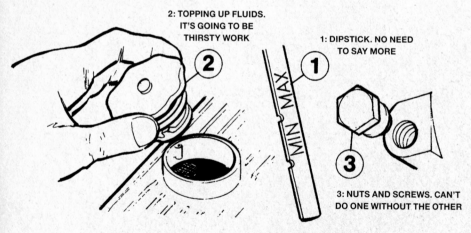

2: TOPPING UP FLUIDS. IT'S GOING TO BE THIRSTY WORK

1: DIPSTICK. NO NEED TO SAY MORE

3: NUTS AND SCREWS. CAN'T DO ONE WITHOUT THE OTHER

FIG 16•2 **CHECKING EVERYTHING'S IN WORKING ORDER BEFORE YOU GET GOING**

b) Glans. The bulb-shaped head. It contains many nerve endings and can provide intense pleasure. Softer and spongier than the shaft (see below), it is ergonomically designed for optimum entry into the XX model.

c) Urethra. Slit at the tip of the glans which emits urine and semen (not at the same time, obviously) in normal operation. It can also emit blood and pus, which is very much not normal operation and requires a visit to the doctor PDQ.

d) Shaft. A complex hydraulic mechanism containing blood vessels and erectile tissue. In times of excitement, blood flows from the brain to these vessels, causing the shaft to stiffen and the brain temporarily to lose some functions. Think of it in the same way countries occasionally relocate their capitals. For many men, the more southern of their two brains makes far more of their (a) decisions (b) bad decisions than the more northern one.

e) Frenulum (aka banjo string): the part which connects the foreskin to the glans. Can be broken, and hurts like absolute buggery when it does (also bleeds like a good 'un too).

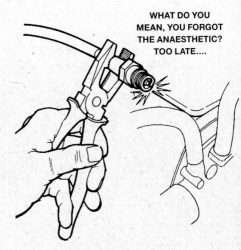

WHAT DO YOU MEAN, YOU FORGOT THE ANAESTHETIC? TOO LATE....

FIG 16•3 **GETTING THE SNIP: MALE VASECTOMY**

f) Coronal ridge. The rim between the glans and shaft. Both the coronal ridge and the frenulum are very sensitive, and not in an 'I'm-here-to-listen-to-all-your-problems kind of way' either.

g) Scrotum. A soft sack attached to the bottom of the shaft which contains two pouches housing a testicle (centre for storing and producing semen) each. (Except for, according to popular musical culture, the case of Adolf Hitler, on whose person only one could be found, with the other rumoured to be in the Albert Hall, Kensington Core, London SW7 2AP.)

XX parts

Female reproductive equipment
Vagina aka pussy, beaver, muff and 74,857 other, more offensive, terms.

As with penises, the Kama Sutra likes to divide vaginas into three categories by size: doe, mare and cow-elephant. It is hard to imagine the last of those being a compliment in this world or indeed any conceivable parallel one.

The terms 'vulva' and 'vagina' are often used either interchangeably or independently to refer to the female genitals en masse, but they are different and separate things. The vulva encompasses the outside of the genitals, where clothes touch skin, and the vagina is the internal corridor leading from the vulva to the uterus. The transition zone between the two is called the vestibule which is also an old-fashioned word for 'hall'. (It would liven up *Downton Abbey* no end if Mrs Patmore invited Carson the butler to meet her in the vestibule.)

The female genitals consist of the following parts:

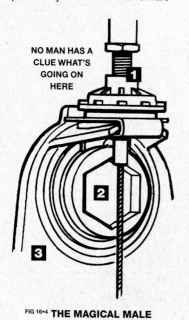

NO MAN HAS A CLUE WHAT'S GOING ON HERE

FIG 16•4 **THE MAGICAL MALE MYSTERY TOUR**

a) **Labia majora, the outer lips.** Two thick vertical lips which stretch all the way from the mons pubis, which sits just above the genitals, to the bottom of the vulva. The outer portion of each lip is usually covered with hair (at least before the waxers have got to work), whereas the inner side is smooth.

b) **Labia minora, the inner lips.** Also vertical, but thinner and resting inside the labia majora (though one or both may protrude beyond them). Contain erectile tissue and nerve endings which are responsive to sexual stimulation. Between the folds at the top of the labia minora can be found the head of the...

c) Clitoris. For most men, the location of the clitoris is up there with how the dishwasher works and the date of their mother-in-law's birthday as the biggest mystery in their lives. (The fabled male refusal to ask for directions at any time and under any circumstances doesn't help either.) The clitoris is the most sensitive and erotically charged part of the female anatomy: it has 8,000 nerve endings, more than twice as many as the head of the penis. (It's often said that the clitoris is the only part designed totally for pleasure, but this isn't quite true: it swells when stimulated and closes the urethra in order to help prevent bladder infection.) The clitoris is like an iceberg (insert your own *Titanic* joke here) in that only a small part of it, the head (itself protected by a hood) appears outside the body, and this head is so sensitive that it often retracts beneath that hood again as a woman nears climax.

d) Urethra. Opening between the clitoris and the vagina which allows urine to be expelled from the bladder. The word 'urethra' is often used both for the opening and the tube itself: the female urethra is much shorter than the male one and therefore more prone to infection.

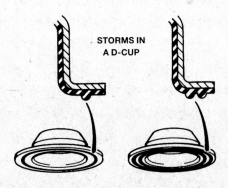

STORMS IN A D-CUP

FIG 16•5 **THANKS FOR THE MAMMARIES**

e) Vagina. Opens within the labia minora just below the urethra and extends into the cervix. At rest, the average vagina is about four inches long and an inch wide, but lengthens, widens and self-lubricates with sexual arousal.

g) G-spot. An area on the front wall of the vagina which is especially sensitive to stimulation. Some experts believe it to be effectively the back end of the clitoris. Named after the German gynaecologist Ernst Gräfenberg, who first 'discovered' it. (He was probably looking for the clitoris at the time, in the same way that Christopher Columbus was looking for India when he found America. 'Yeah, this is what I was trying to find all along. It was, OK? It was. Shut up. Just shut up.')

Sat Nav

In the olden days, finding a sexual partner was easy. You found someone who lived within half a mile of you, checked that you weren't related to them, and off you went. But the world has got smaller since then, and there are now such a dizzying array of ways to meet people that you'd be forgiven for not knowing where to start.

And that, my friend, is where Haynes Explains comes in. Here are some common places to find that special someone (or, failing that, simply that undiscerning someone), with positives and negatives mapped out for each:

1. Public transport

👍 lots of people, therefore lots of choice. Usually delayed, which means plenty of time to get to know someone.

👎 the unwritten British rule that forbids people from talking to strangers on public transport. Remember the horror that greeted the Tube chat badges a few years ago, where people were offered badges to wear signifying they were happy to talk to strangers on the London Underground? Only drunks, lunatics and Americans talk on the Tube. Everyone else stares at their shoes in resentful silence.

2. In a library/bookshop

👍 it makes you look intelligent and sensitive, being somewhere like this. If the object of your affection is holding or reading a book, that's a conversation opener right there. Many bookshops now have a café attached, so you can go for a coffee without needing to leave the building (i.e. before they have second thoughts).

👎 most libraries have been closed down now. Hanging out by the 'railway history' section is not going to make you look like a suave, debonair, international man of mystery.

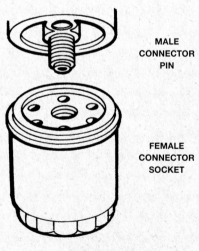

MALE CONNECTOR PIN

FEMALE CONNECTOR SOCKET

FIG 16•6 **YOUR SEXUAL MANOEUVRES IN THE DARK**

SWIPE RIGHT:
YES PLEASE,
ME LIKE THE
LOOK OF YOU

SWIPE
LEFT: NO
THANKS.
NEXT!

FIG 16•7 **THE ONLINE SWIPING DICHOTOMY**

3. Walking the dog

👍 There's a reason Hollywood movies feature dog walking as a meet cute for wannabe couples, and that's pretty obvious: dogs are (in general) adorable, and they give the humans walking them the chance to chat while they sniff each other's arses (the dogs, obviously, not the humans. Not yet, at any rate. And certainly not mid-morning on Clapham Common).

👎 Your chances of a first date, let alone a second, will go out of the window the moment your larger, more aggressive dog tries to savage their smaller, more timid one. And even if the dogs get on as well as the humans, there are few things less sexy than clutching poop bags full of their intended purpose in life.

4. Online

👍 Choice, for a start: literally anyone and everyone with a smartphone and no significant other (though the second half of that is certainly optional, judging by the amount of attached men and women on dating sites). The ease of swiping left or right, which – in theory at least – reduces the waste on both parties' time by weeding out the obviously incompatible.

👎 Jeez, where to start? There is no limit to the amount of crazy out there. Anyone who's been online dating for more than five minutes will have their share of horror stories. The fact that someone's profile photo is (a) 10 years out of date (b) not even of them is only the beginning. Everyone is either a compulsive liar (no, mate, you're not off to the Maldives tomorrow), brutally honest (me? You're no oil painting yourself, sunshine), or both.

WARNING

Dick pics. Pictures of Dick Emery, Dick Francis, Dick van Dyke and Dick Cheney are acceptable, though if you send them, the recipient will just think you're a bit weird. But the more usual use of the phrase: no. If someone wants to see it, they'll ask.

The handbrake

Consent

There's a lot about sex which is funny, either deliberately or inadvertently, but consent is not one of them. Consent is no laughing matter, not in the slightest. Like many things which you might think should go without saying, actually consent needs saying again and again, and Haynes Explains is not going to apologise for stressing this bit as much as it can.

No one should ever be forced to have sexual contact, however you choose to define it, against their will. Consent has to be given, not assumed, and the absence of active consent is and should always be taken as refusal. Consent doesn't have to be verbal – it's pretty obvious when someone likes you and is keen to have sex – but by the same token lack of consent can also be verbal or non-verbal.

Things that mean yes:

Saying 'yes', ripping the other person's clothes off, demanding with either vocal or body language that you take things further.

Things that mean no:

'No,' 'I'm not sure,' 'Maybe later', 'I don't like the idea of that', 'I'm with someone,' 'I like you, but…', 'Leave me alone,' 'You're not my type,' 'piss off', silence. Silence is a big 'no', whether it's simply because she doesn't want to or because she's asleep, unconscious, too drunk/stoned to speak, or similar. Someone who can't speak cannot give consent, and without consent you cannot have sex with them: end of, no ifs, no buts. And of course by definition anyone under the age of consent cannot give consent.

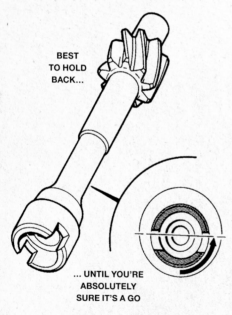

BEST TO HOLD BACK...

... UNTIL YOU'RE ABSOLUTELY SURE IT'S A GO

FIG 16•8 **YOU CAN NEVER BE TOO CAREFUL WITH CONSENT**

⚠ Consent through the FRIES mnemonic

Freely given, without pressure or manipulation

If you ask someone for sex 49 times and they say 'yes' on the 50th, that's not consent. You should have stopped at the first 'no.'

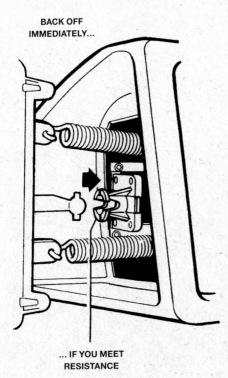

BACK OFF
IMMEDIATELY...

... IF YOU MEET
RESISTANCE

FIG 16•9 **MAKE SURE FRIES
SPRINGS TO MIND**

Reversible

Anyone can change their mind anytime. Doesn't matter if you're mid-act or if you've done it 100 times before.

Informed

You can only properly consent if you have all the relevant information. Someone saying they'll wear a condom but doesn't, someone who knows (or even thinks) they're carrying an STI but doesn't tell you, someone who has a partner or spouse but conveniently forgets to mention them – full consent can't be given in any of these situations.

Enthusiastic

Someone should only do stuff they want to do, not what they feel pressured into. They should enter into anything on their own terms or not at all. If a woman doesn't want to go down on a man that's her right, even if he's gone down on her.

Specific

Consenting to one thing doesn't mean consenting to everything. Kissing someone doesn't mean consent to full sex; consenting to vaginal sex doesn't imply consent to anal sex; consenting to a blindfold doesn't imply consenting to handcuffs and fetish gear.

The starter motor

Getting in the mood for sex isn't simply a question of turning up and saying 'you ready?' Actually, scratch that. For 50% of the population it's exactly that. But for the other 50% – the fairer, more intelligent 50%, naturally – it's a longer and more complicated process which involves some or all of the following stages:

1. Alcohol

We're talking a glass or two max here, not a dozen Jagerbombs with Bacardi Breezer chasers. The latter will get you in the mood too, of course, but it will also get you an emperor-sized hangover and dim, fleeting memories of having done something – more than one thing, probably – that you bitterly regret the next day.

2. Massage

The great thing about massage is that it's both relaxing and arousing, and therefore provides a perfect bridge between, er, not having sex and having sex. It all depends on the kind of massage, of course. Soft and tender is good. Being pummelled as though in a Turkish bath or the clinic of a particularly sadistic chiropractor is not.

3. Bath

Long and hot and scented candles, if that's your thing. Shave your legs: it can feel sensual and will look great. Stay in long enough to be fully relaxed. Don't stay in so long that your skin wrinkles and you look like a prune.

4. Fantasise

Preferably about the person you'll be having sex with later. If need be, read or watch something erotic, but not for too long: it may or may not be a great start to the evening if you begin the date by saying 'can you wait a few minutes, it's just getting to the good bit?'

5. Put on sexy lingerie

Again, preferably your own.

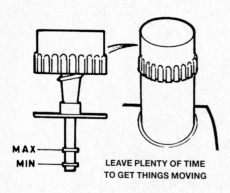

MAX
MIN — LEAVE PLENTY OF TIME TO GET THINGS MOVING

FIG 16•10 **PRIMING THE PUMPS**

Kiss chase

Kissing is at once the start of sex in most cases and also one of the most intimate aspects of it (indeed, in many situations such as threesomes and paid sex work, participants like to adopt a 'no kissing' rule. There are few things sexier than being a good kisser (and being known as a good kisser). Haynes Explains has done some selfless research to bring you some tips on how to achieve this.

a) Keep your breath fresh, obviously. Mints, chewing gum, toothpaste and mouthwash are your friends here. Plenty of things can cause bad breath: not just things like smoking, alcohol, spicy food and gum disease, but one of the most common causes is dehydration.

b) Tease. Kissing round the neck and ears can be just as erotic as kissing on the mouth. As for curling your tongue up and putting it in the other person's ear... for some reason men tend to love this and women tend to hate it. Be warned.

c) Don't be a soggy kisser. If the other person wants to feel what it's like to be dripping with saliva, they'll go and cuddle a jowly bloodhound.

d) Don't kiss too forcefully right from the off unless the sexual tension between you is so strong that you could, to pick a phrase from the cliché trolley, cut it with a knife. Passionately aggressive snogs are great in the plateau phase (and there's something extraordinarily sexy about people who kiss well in the middle of hot sex) but to go from 0 to 60 with the kiss is unwise. Build.

e) Use the tongue wisely. The two most common complaints about bad kissers is either that they just let their tongue lie there like a dead fish on the slab or they whirl it around the other person's mouth like a washing machine on boilwash setting. Neither technique is in any way sexy. Change the rhythm from fast to slow, deep to shallow, and back again.

Think of kissing like a handshake. There are the ones that are way too hard and the ones that are way too limp. Kiss with the relaxed confidence of someone who gives a proper handshake.

Mirror, signal, manoeuvre

'Sex act' is usually ghastly tabloid speak for something the newspaper thinks its readers are too innocent and puritanical to have spelled out in full (despite the fact that the vast majority of those readers would hardly raise an eyebrow and probably do far more exciting/transgressive things in the privacy of their own homes on a regular basis). But the phrase speaks of a tendency to parcel sex up into separate and discrete entities, whereas it should be – and at its best is – all part of the same thing. Take the word 'foreplay', which suggests that it's just an amuse-bouche, a waypoint on the way to intercourse, whereas for

many people, and especially many women, it can be just as if not more satisfying than what most people consider 'actual sex'.

Both men and women go through the same four phases of the sexual response cycle: excitement, plateau, orgasm and resolution. The difference is that men often go through them more quickly, and in some cases much more quickly. It can be reminiscent of the cartoon featuring a chicken and an egg in bed together. The chicken has a blissful smile and is smoking a cigarette, while the egg looks furious as it hisses 'well, I guess that answers the question.'

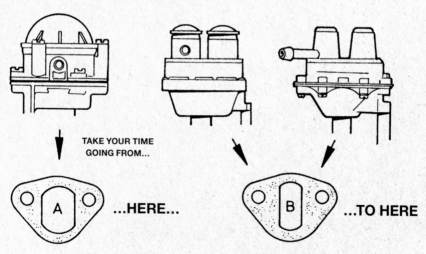

TAKE YOUR TIME GOING FROM...

...HERE...   ...TO HERE

FIG 16•11 **A TO B: THE SCENIC ROUTE**

⚠ The four phases

Phase 1 Excitement, both men and women will see their heart rate and breathing accelerate, their skin becoming flushed and nipples erect, and the blood flow to their genitals increasing. The man's penis and testicles swell and his scrotum tightens; the woman's clitoris, labia minora and vaginal walls begin to swell, vaginal lubrication begins and her breasts become fuller.

Phase 2 Plateau, sees an intensification of the changes in phase 1 as orgasm approaches. The man's testicles tighten; the woman's vagina continues to swell, her vaginal walls turn a dark purple, and her clitoris becomes so sensitive that it retracts under the clitoral hood again. It is towards the end of this phase that one or both parties inform Jesus Christ in no uncertain terms that they're coming.

Phase 3 Orgasm, is the shortest phase of the cycle, generally lasting only a few seconds. Both men and women experience involuntary muscle contractions in their genitals. Men will usually ejaculate semen, though not always (it is possible for a man to orgasm without ejaculating or ejaculate without orgasming). Women may ejaculate fluid – 'squirting' – though most do not. Several different types of female orgasm have been identified: the clitoral, the vaginal (only around a third of women can come through penile penetration alone), the G-spot, the cervical, the urethral, the anal, the breast, the all-over body, the oral (that is, women having an orgasm from having their own mouth stimulated) and the mental. Feel inadequate yet, chaps?

Phase 4 Resolution (which makes it sound like an agreement reached between management and trade unions at the eleventh hour to avoid industrial action, and let's be honest, we've all had sex like that at least once), the body slowly returns to its normal level of functioning as the sexual swelling subsides. This phase is characterised by a feeling of intimacy and well-being (if you're a woman) and deep fatigue alleviated only by turning on Sky Sports (if you're a man). Some women can return to the orgasm phase with further stimulation and have multiple orgasms, but men need a recovery time (known as a refractory period) before they can reach orgasm again. This period varies not just from man to man but also by age. In late teens and early twenties it can be a few minutes; by middle age it can be a few days with no heavy exercise in between and can you bring my slippers if you're up there, darling?

Travelling abroad

The late, great Barry White, when asked the strangest place he'd ever had sex, replied 'there ain't nowhere Barry White ain't had sex. Washing machines, fire engines, armoured cars: you name it, Barry White's done it there. The only place Barry White ain't had sex is the moon, and that's 'cos Barry White ain't been to the moon.' Aside from the bonus points for referring to himself in the third person, the best thing about this is the implication that, if only NASA were to restart the Apollo programme at vast expense to the public purse, then Bazza could get it on in one-sixth gravity and we'd all be happy.

There are many places to have sex: some of them good, others bad. Haynes Explains has endeavoured to sort the wheat from the chaff, so to speak.

The Good...

Bed
Obviously. A little boring, perhaps, but there are plenty of reasons why the common or garden bed is still the go-to location for sex: comfort, privacy and no commute to the sleep zone afterwards.

Outdoors
This depends where, obviously. An isolated lakeshore on a summer evening is good. IKEA car park on a Bank Holiday Monday is bad.

Cinema
An arthouse movie near the end of its run, the back row of a nearly or wholly deserted auditorium: relive those teenage fumblings (but better this time).

Kitchen
What else is a kitchen island for? (Well, lots, come to think if it, but you know what we mean.) Make sure that all hot surfaces are turned off and all sharp objects out of reach, as (a) it'll hurt if you don't (b) whatever explanation you give, the doctors in A & E won't believe you.

Laundry room
Use the vibrations and warmth of the washing machine on a high-temperature cotton cycle for best effect. By 'laundry room', of course, we mean your own laundry room or area in your house, not a public laundrette. This isn't a Levi's ad and Nick Kamen won't be there.

The Bad...

Shower Oh, it sounds great. But you've got to get the temperature right, and unless it's an enormous power shower then there won't be room for both of you under the water flow, and deep down you don't really know whether you should be having sex or showering, and there's no real etiquette for who passes the shampoo to who mid-coitus, and... listen, shower in the shower and have sex somewhere else.

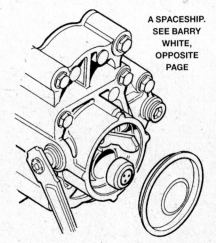

A SPACESHIP. SEE BARRY WHITE, OPPOSITE PAGE

FIG 16•12 **APOLLO 19: WALRUS OF LOVE**

Sauna Another one which sounds great in theory but turns out to be a terrible idea in practice. Saunas (and their bastard cousin the steam room) are quite hot and sweaty enough without needing two people adding to it. Trying to get a grip on each other in situations like this is like trying to grapple with a buttered pig.

Aeroplane bathroom The Mile High Club, right? Wrong. They're cramped, they're full of enough germs and bacteria to make a biological weapon, there's a queue of people who've gone overboard on the inflight Chardonnay and need to evacuate it, and your wife's in seat 23B and wondering what's taking you so long.

Roaring fireplace Yes, very romantic: a deep sheepskin rug, the firelight catching your lover's face in gentle tones of orange, yellow and red. But get too close and the only nuts roasting on an open fire will be your own.

Beach Sand everywhere, and we mean everywhere. Waves which knock you off your feet and half-drown you when you try to get up. You think it'll be like Burt Lancaster and Deborah Kerr in *From Here To Eternity*. Actually it'll be like the last scene in *Point Break* when Patrick Swayze takes on the giant wave and loses.

Driving position

There's a seemingly endless list of possible sexual positions, but in essence all of them are variations on one of six themes.

1. Man On Top
Also known as the missionary, after the South Seas natives who preferred women on top, sitting and rear entry positions and were startled to see Western missionaries adopting this

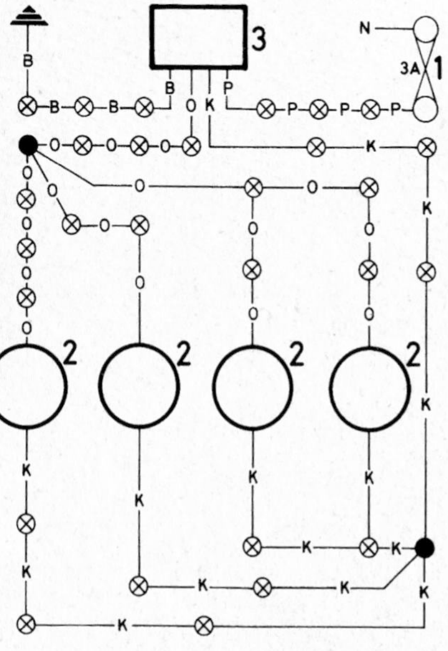

FIG 16•13 **SEXUAL POSITIONS. FOLLOWED BY OSTEOPATH POSITIONS**

one. The missionary has many things going for it: It allows full body contact and for both partners to maintain eye contact and kiss throughout the sex. Men can control the depth of their penetration and the speed of their thrust. Many women say they like this position as it makes them feel safe and protected. Besides, if they get bored it's easy to whip out their phone and check their social media feeds over their partner's shoulder.

2. Woman On Top
In this position the woman can control the depth of penetration and the speed of the thrusting. Many men find this position particularly arousing as, when the woman raises herself, they get to see their partner's naked torso and can either reach up to feel her breasts and/ or use their fingers on her clitoris as she rides them.

3. Side By Side
Since penetration is not as deep here, it can be more comfortable for women whose lovers have large penises. Men can thrust for longer without climaxing.

4. Rear Entry
Arguably the most animalistic of positions (as evidenced by use of the phrase 'doggy-style', and back in the

days of the Kama Sutra it was known as 'the cow'. The Kama Sutra goes on to say that 'one can imitate other animals, mounting the woman like an ass, playing with her like a cat, attacking like a tiger, stamping like an elephant, pawing the ground like a pig, riding horse-fashion. Thus, one learns a thousand ways to copulate.' And all this long before *Wildlife On One* was a twinkle in David Attenborough's eye. Both men and women can find this position highly charged, with women enjoying the depth of penetration and the feeling of being 'taken'. On the negative side, it doesn't allow for much mid-sex kissing unless you're Olympic-gymnast-level flexible.

5. Standing

Good in times of necessity (the old 'knee-trembler' of Victorian prostitutes servicing their clients up against a wall). Indeed, the woman is probably best using a wall to brace herself unless she is very light and/or the man is very strong. If the woman wraps her legs around the man, ask her to remove her stilettos first or else he'll end up looking like some poor schoolkid given thirty lashes by a sadistic headmaster, *Tom Brown's School Days*-style.

6. Sitting/Kneeling

Access your inner Gandhi. Except his USP was that he didn't do much of this stuff.

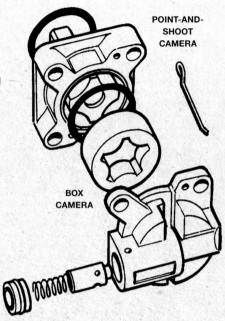

POINT-AND-SHOOT CAMERA

BOX CAMERA

FIG 16•14 **CAMERA OBSCURA: SEXUAL POSITIONS FOR THE ADVANCED PRACTITIONER**

WARNING

There are some well-known variations on these positions, all of them demanding greater or lesser degrees of dexterity and flexibility: take your pick from the Reverse Cowgirl, Hovering Butterfly, Butter-Churner, Stand And Deliver, Wheelbarrow, Spider and Passion Propeller.

Servicing

Oral sex can be a battleground. Some people (of both sexes) refuse to do it at all. Others expect to receive it but don't like giving it. Still others will happily give it but don't like receiving it. And, of course, there are lots of people very happy with oral sex in all its forms. The Kama Sutra, a little surprisingly, is not overly down with oral sex from men to women, and only endorses blow jobs from three categories of women: promiscuous ones, servants and those who do arduous work. (That 21st-century

woke reworking of the Kama Sutra clearly still needs work.)

There are in essence only two types of men: those who enjoy blow jobs, and those who are dead. The extent to which women enjoy giving blow jobs is a different matter: as Samantha in *Sex and the City* said, 'honey, they don't call it a job for nothing'. All kinds of things may be going through her head while she's giving head: the fact that he needs new boxer shorts, how much her jaw's hurting, why nature couldn't have designed the penis to be better-

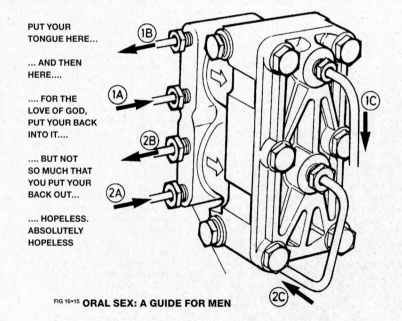

PUT YOUR TONGUE HERE...

... AND THEN HERE....

.... FOR THE LOVE OF GOD, PUT YOUR BACK INTO IT....

.... BUT NOT SO MUCH THAT YOU PUT YOUR BACK OUT...

.... HOPELESS. ABSOLUTELY HOPELESS

FIG 16•15 **ORAL SEX: A GUIDE FOR MEN**

looking and don't even get her started on the testicles, whether looking up at him will be sexy or creepy, how much hand to use, what was that exact technique in *Cosmo* a few months back, and of course the final four-way decision: spit, swallow, boobs or face?

Put that way, it's amazing that any woman ever agrees to it in the first place.

That said, in general men have far fewer complaints about the way women perform oral sex than vice versa. Call it what you want - carpet-munching, drinking from the furry cup, dining at the 'Y', going south, muff-diving, tipping the velvet, yodelling in the canyon or scores of others – here are some dos and don't's. It's harder to please a woman with oral sex than it is a man, but she will never forget those who manage it.

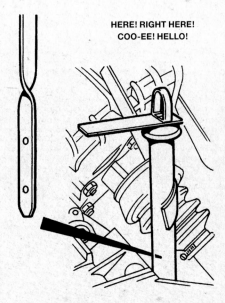

HERE! RIGHT HERE! COO-EE! HELLO!

FIG 16•16 **CLITORAL LOCATION: ANOTHER GUIDE FOR MEN**

a) Start slowly and pay attention to the labia. This will stimulate blood flow and increase her excitement.

b) Take her to the brink before bringing her back. Repeat this a few times.

c) Ensure that you have a variety of tongue moves rather than simple licking. Spelling out letters on her clitoris, if done well, can drive her wild. 'The quick brown fox jumps over the lazy dog' and all that. Capitalise, italicise and change the font if you're really feeling adventurous. Some women like the sensation of a man humming while he's going down on her.

d) Keep a light, slow touch on her clitoris unless she tells you otherwise.

Don't assume that every woman is the same. They're not. What works for one will leave another totally cold and vice versa.

Added extras

As with sex positions, there's an impressive array of ways to spice up your sex life with costumes, toys, kinks and BDSM. Kink communities are very big into avoiding 'kink-shaming', and like to work with two maxims: YKINMKBYKIO (which sounds like an obscure prefecture in central Japan but actually stands for 'your kink is not my kink but your kink is okay') and 'squick', which means something which you personally find uncomfortable/repulsive/disgusting while still recognising that other people can enjoy it.

Costumes

Leaving aside the obvious ones (nurse, French maid, secretary, superheroes, fireman etc.), people have reported being asked to dress up in all the following, and rest assured that this is only the tip of the iceberg:

a) like Bruce Willis in Die Hard (dirty vest, fake blood, bare feet)
b) football shirts
c) wedding dresses
d) as a therapist, including couch
e) as a Scotsman, with full kilt and wee-Jimmy tartan hat.

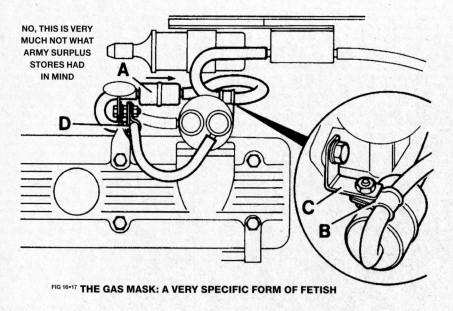

NO, THIS IS VERY MUCH NOT WHAT ARMY SURPLUS STORES HAD IN MIND

FIG 16•17 **THE GAS MASK: A VERY SPECIFIC FORM OF FETISH**

Dogging

Basically, have sex in public and/or watch others do so. Thought to be named after either the idea of 'dogging' couples having sex (i.e. following them close enough to watch them) or through people using the idea of walking the dog as an excuse to participate. 'Just off out with the dog, darling. I'll be back in four hours. Yes, he does need a lot of exercise these days. No, I don't know why I keep getting grass stains on my trousers.'

This being the 21st century, there are a host of helpful websites telling you where you can find dogging sites near you. Technically, dogging can be a criminal offence, but in practice the police's policy is that of a 'gradual

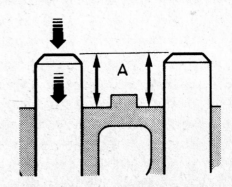

FIG 16·18 **ENSURE YOUR SHOCK ABSORBERS ARE IN GOOD NICK BEFORE DOGGING**

approach, with arrests being seen very much as a last resort' (i.e. we're going to try and catch some real criminals and/or PC Johnson's missus is often in the layby off the A356 and we don't want him finding out).

⚠ Dogging Dos and Don'ts

✔ **Do** stay anonymous: create a dogging name to protect your identity.

✔ **Do** agree a signal or safe word in case someone wants to stop.

✔ **Do** flash your interior light if you're happy for people to watch.

✔ **Do** Roll down your window or open the door if you want people to come closer or join in.

✘ **Don't** do it anywhere where children or unsuspecting adults could come across it.

✘ **Don't** trespass, disturb the peace or give any reason for the police to come.

✘ **Don't** turn up alone if you're a woman.

✘ **Don't** touch (if watching) unless specifically invited to do so.

BDSM

Think of BDSM and you probably think either of the old adage 'sticks and stones may break my bones, but whips and chains excite me' or of *Fifty Shades of Grey*, in which E.L. James made untold millions off the back of a hitherto unsuspected penchant among housewives for indulging in a little light bondage fantasy involving a devastatingly handsome billionaire (which in fairness rules out most actual real-life billionaires). The BDSM community have little time for the book that made them famous, pointing out its many inaccuracies (not to mention the fact that they never asked to be famous in the first place).

BDSM is actually a catch-all term for three separate categories: BD (Bondage/Discipline), DS (Dominance/Submission) and SM (Sadism/Masochism). Any given situation can contain one, two or all three elements, and in each interaction there's a top and bottom: the one who gives and the one who receives. If this sounds like a recipe for unbridled pain, BDSMers will

WARNING

BDSM is not for everyone, and nor is it for beginners. Obviously everyone has to start somewhere, but if you are interested then seek out someone experienced to help you become acquainted with the scene and its rules.

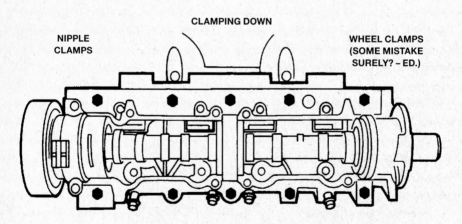

NIPPLE CLAMPS

CLAMPING DOWN

WHEEL CLAMPS (SOME MISTAKE SURELY? – ED.)

FIG 16•19 **THE RESTRAINTS OF THE TRADE**

tell you that nothing could be further from the truth.

First, both parties spend time beforehand discussing exactly what they will and won't allow. In this respect, consent is much more freely given and understood than it often is in 'normal' sex (or vanilla sex, as BDSMers call it). The acronym SSC – safe, sane and consensual – is widely heard. There are hard limits – places beyond which they won't go – and safe words which instantly call a halt to proceedings. (Safe words can't be ones which might be called out in the heat of the moment, and indeed part of the thrill for some participants is to beg for mercy or cessation knowing it will be refused. 'Red light' is a common safe word.) And there's also an emphasis on aftercare, where the participants discuss the experience and check that the other one enjoyed it.

An interesting point about BDSM is that, though tops appear to be calling the shots, it's actually bottoms who are in control: they're the ones who can use the safe word and bring proceedings to an immediate halt.

Toys

Toys come in all shapes and sizes, quite literally. There are dildos (not be confused with Dido, the dodo, or Dilbert); vibrators (which make it easy for a woman to orgasm for three main reasons – the intensity of the vibration, the fact that most use is done when alone and therefore relaxed, and that she knows exactly where to place the stimulation and at what intensity); butt plugs and anal beads (the first being effectively a dildo for the anus, and beads being inserted and then pulled out just before or at the moment of orgasm); and, for the discerning chap, a cock ring which reduces blood flow away from the penis and therefore leads to firmer and longer-lasting erections.

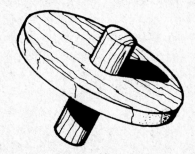

FIG 16•20 **TOO LATE, NEANDERTHAL MAN REALISED THAT THIS WAS SUPPOSED TO BE A WHEEL**

Troubleshooting

Sex is in general good for your health. It raises the heart rate, which in turn helps to lower blood pressure and improves overall cardiovascular fitness. It can also reduce headaches (a little ironic, perhaps, given that 'I've got a headache' is such a go-to excuse for avoiding sex), help with insomnia and ease tension and stress. It helps keep your immune system running well, fights colds and flu, boosts your libido (the more you get, the more you want), improves bladder control, can lower the risk of heart attacks and prostate cancer, can make you look younger (unless of course you are in the throes of no-sleep-sex-till-dawn sessions, in which case you'll look 105 BUT IT'LL BE WORTH IT), and improves your all-round sense of well-being.

But with the S of sex comes the TD of transmitted diseases. Watch out for these bad boys:

1. Chlamydia
Often called the silent STD because by the time you notice the symptoms the disease is already well-advanced. Infection in the urethra can make urination painful (the technical term is 'bloody hell, mate, I feel like I'm pissing barbed wire here'). In women it can cause a bacterial infection deep within the fallopian tubes which in turn can lead to chronic pain and even infertility.

2. Gonorrhoea
Aka 'the clap', though God knows there's little worth applauding here. Like chlamydia, it can often go undetected until damage has already

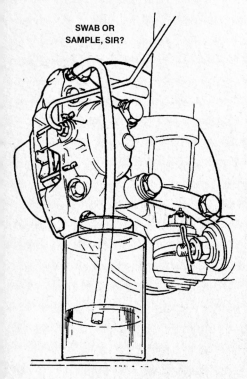

SWAB OR SAMPLE, SIR?

FIG 16•21 **LABORATORY TESTING APPARATUS**

occurred. In men, symptoms can include a yellow pus-like discharge known as gleet, which is rather magnificently onomatopoeic: even if you didn't know what gleet was, you wouldn't have it pegged as A Good Thing just from the name.

3. Syphilis

'You don't hear much about syphilis these days,' opined the character Tom Wamsgans in the HBO series *Succession*. 'Very much the MySpace of STDs.' Apart from being the kind of line so good that whoever wrote it surely shut up their laptop for the day and went to the pub, it's not quite true: syphilis is making a comeback, and not in an 80s band we're-just-here-to-top-up-the-pension-pot-and-then-we'll-go-away-again kind of way. Left untreated, syphilis can be fatal, and at the very least cause serious damage (including madness – and, talking of 80s bands, not Suggs' mob either).

4. Herpes

There are two types of herpes virus: herpes simplex 1, which occurs orally and looks like cold sores, and herpes simplex 2, which occurs genitally and manifests as bumps or blisters around the penis or vagina. Herpes simplex 10, which Eddie Murphy references to get round a snooty maître d' in *Beverly Hills Cop*, does not exist.

WHAT A & E WON'T THANK YOU FOR....

FIG 16•22 ... **PARTICULARLY ON A BUSY FRIDAY NIGHT**

5. HPV

The human papilloma virus, also known as condyloma, can cause genital warts, which are every bit as ugly bugly as they sound. There are five common types of HPV that are associated with cervical cancer, but these strains are not the ones which cause genital warts. HPV is basically a smorgasbord of different strains: an ensemble cast, a supergroup.

6. HIV/AIDS

Once fatal, of course, but thankfully no longer thanks to retroviral drugs. HIV and AIDS are not the same thing. HIV, the human immunodeficiency virus, is a precursor to AIDS, acquired immune deficiency syndrome. You can have HIV without it ever transmuting into full-blown AIDS, but you can't have AIDS without first having HIV. HIV attacks the immune system, leaving the body unable to fight off common sicknesses or other diseases.

Glossary

Phrase	Meaning
ABC sex	especially of long-term couples, to have sex only on anniversaries, birthdays and Christmas.
Asexual	people who do not experience sexual attraction.
Benching	keeping someone on the subs' bench: that is, not into someone enough to officially commit to them, but into them enough not to want them to find someone else. The benchee should of course turn round and tell the bencher to, ahem, go forth and multiply.
Bicurious	those exploring whether or not they're attracted to people of the same gender as well as those of another gender. A sort of try-before-you-buy (or, more accurately, try-before-you're-bi).
Catfishing	to pretend to be someone else online.
Cisgender	those whose assigned sex and gender identity coincide (that is, the majority of people.)
Cuffing season	the period of autumn and winter when people hook up with the nearest vaguely presentable person around in order not to have to spend long cold nights alone. Such relationships end the moment the temperature begins to rise again.
Demisexual	people who only experience sexual attraction in certain situations, e.g. after forming a strong emotional connection with someone. Not to be confused with Demi Moore, especially if you've read her rather eye-opening autobiography.
DTR	Define The Relationship. The conversation between two people at some stage in a relationship where they, well, define that relationship. Can go wrong if one person thinks it's true love while the other has been making Casanova look like The 40 Year Old Virgin.
Emergency call	pre-arranged call from a friend detailing a fictitious emergency which allows you to extricate yourself from a terrible date.
Friends With Benefits	friends who sleep with each other now and then but aren't in a committed relationship.

Gender fluid	someone who feels themselves a mix of male and female, but perhaps to different extents on different days. Any other interpretation of the word 'fluid' is just your imagination, you filthy, wicked child.
Ghosting	to cut all contact with someone you're dating without telling them. Refuse to take calls, answer texts, social media messages etc. A deeply, deeply unpleasant thing to do.
Jackintosh	a computer used exclusively for porn.
Kittenfishing	basically catfishing lite. You don't pretend to be someone else, but you present a version of yourself so idealised as to be misleading: a photo many years out of date, ridiculous exaggerations of personal and professional achievement (e.g. 'multiple Ironman' to make people think you've done the world's hardest triathlon many times when actually all you've done is watched Robert Downey Jr. as Tony Stark over and again).
LGBTQ	shorthand for all those who aren't straight. Lesbian, Gay, Bisexual, Transgender and Queer/Questioning.
Netflix And Chill	euphemism for sex. As in 'why don't you come over and we can watch some Netflix and chill?'
Pansexual	someone attracted to members of all gender identities or expressions. Basically, someone who will never go home alone on a Saturday night. Not to be confused with the god Pan (though he was a bit of a goer himself), kitchen pans, or pan pipes played in cheap restaurants by guys in ponchos who want you to think they're Peruvian but are actually from Croydon.
Polyamorous	people who have consensual relationships with multiple partners. Very much of the have cake/eat cake school, and good luck to them.
Procrasturbating	using masturbation to while away time when you should be doing something more urgent.
Stealthing	of a man, to remove a condom during sex without telling his partner. Not cool.
Transgender	someone who has transitioned or is transitioning from male to female (or vice versa), or someone who is biologically one sex but identifies as another.
Trisexual	will try anything sexual. (We may have just made this up.)

Selling your vehicle

Paul Simon sang about the 50 ways to leave your lover, but sometimes it's not as simple as that. Often when relationships end, it's not so much a clean break as a compound fracture. Sex with an ex is not exactly uncommon, but is it a good idea?

Your mileage may vary on this one, and there's no definitive right or wrong answer. Rather than think just about the sex, maybe it's better to consider the reasons behind wanting to have sex with your ex. If you – and they – are clear-eyed enough to be honest about these reasons, you will both be better equipped to work out whether or not you should go for it. (Warning: Dutch courage and/or late-night decision-making don't necessarily aid such clear-eyed honesty.) In the meantime, here are some reasons for and against.

YES

 You know each other's bodies so well that there's little or no awkwardness, and you can just slip back into old routines.

 It can give you an ego boost when you need one.

If it's been a while since you split, it can demystify the relationship and make you realise that neither the sex nor the ex were as good as you thought they were.

It's a low-risk, high-yield investment. No need for expensive dates and the possibility of rejection and/or incompatibility at the end of this particular rainbow. Just dial 1-800-BOOTYCALL and you're good to go.

NO

It doesn't help you really move on and find another partner.

It's too easy to slip back into the patterns of the relationship. There were reasons why you broke up, and they almost certainly haven't gone away. It's called a break-up for a good reason: because it was broken.

 It opens up old wounds and can spark drama that you don't need.

If you're doing it just to prove they still 'need' you, that's not an especially good reason.

 It can lead to shame and confusion afterwards.

Conclusion

Sex is most often an experience for two people, but odd numbers also apply.

Fiat Uno. The celibate, willingly or otherwise: those who, to paraphrase Woody Allen, at least always have sex with someone they love. Celibacy can be a lifelong commitment or a temporary one (such as until the celibate gets married).

There are lots of reasons to be celibate. The most obvious, perhaps, is religious: plenty of denominations across many religions advocate celibacy. The positives of this are that the celibates can enjoy an exclusively spiritual life and, since they don't have to love one person above all others, they can love everyone equally. The negatives are that for many people it's unnatural and, denied the chance to express their sexuality within the confines of a mutually supportive adult relationship, they can turn to child abuse and similar.

Not that you have to be religious to swear off sex for good. Some people just decide their lives are better off without it, particularly if they've had bad experiences in relationships.

Some decide that they'd rather focus on their own personal development alone rather than alongside a partner, some make the decision on medical grounds, and some swear off sex if their sexual behaviour has got out of hand.

Then there are the 'incels', the involuntary celibates: that is, those who would like to have sex and/or a relationship but can't find anyone willing to reciprocate. The word 'incel' may sound like a brand of computer processor or a prescription ointment, but the incel culture is not a nice one. Online incel forums can be toxic swamps of misogyny, racism, self-loathing, entitlement and, most notoriously, incitement to violence: incels have carried out several mass shootings in the USA.

BMW 3 series. Threesome, *ménage a trois*, call it what you will: the threesome is high up there in most people's fantasies (though you can guarantee that if it's a male fantasy then it will almost certainly involve two women; if it's a female fantasy, it is as likely also to involve two women as it is two men).

Titles in the Haynes Explains series

Now that Haynes has explained Sex, you can progress to our full size manuals on car maintenance (a little TLC will keep that running smoothly too), *Men's Cooking Manual* (the way to a woman's heart?), *Shed Manual* (make your own love shack), *Sleep Manual* (so long as it's not on the job), *Vinyl Manual* (a bit of background music).

There are Haynes manuals on just about everything
– but let us know if we've missed one.

Haynes.com